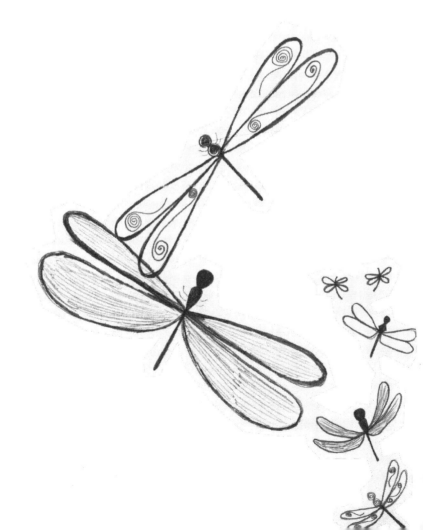

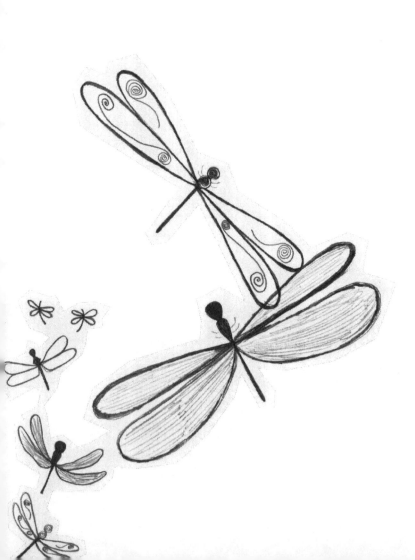

All Things Dance Like Dragonflies

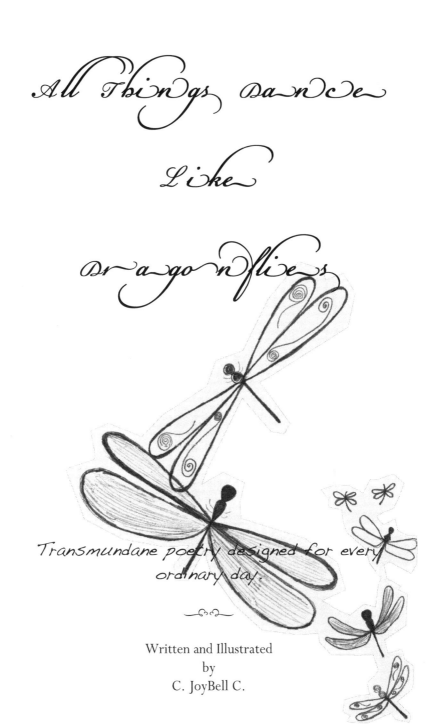

Transmundane poetry designed for every ordinary day.

Written and Illustrated
by
C. JoyBell C.

A third generation artisan of flowery and beadish things, first generation
dragonfly-chaser, one-man kind of woman (for ten years now), die-hard feline-
lover, incessant reader and dreamer of all things Hawaiian, *Ms. Laura Habel* is
the newest addition to the C. JoyBell C. adventure, and completely responsible
for the dragonfly on the cover of this book! She accepts inquiries and praises at
this address: heartinhawaii@mail.com and visitors to this address:
flickr.com/heartinhawaii.

All books by C. JoyBell C. are printed in
the U.S.A., Great Britain,
and Continental Europe.

ISBN: **1482010321**
ISBN- **978-1482010329**

www .cjoybellc.com
authorcjoybellc@gmail.com

Dedication

To everyone who has spent an afternoon in their
childhood catching dragonflies, to every child who hears
the voice of the roses, and to every person awaiting a
new beginning.

My beloved son Gilead, you are the apple of my eye!

The dragonflies never left you! Stop and think about it- they are in the glimmer of your eye, the smell of mists after a rainfall, the memories you almost capture, the sound of how cinnamon falls on your plate... in your darkest hours, and in your brightest ones...dragonflies.

Introduction

The dragonfly is an ancient insect that is steeped in symbolism, which spans out over many cultures and continents. In Japan, the dragonfly is revered as a symbol of speed, agility, victory, happiness, courage and strength! The Japanese also associate the dragonfly with the seasons of summer and autumn and as we can all see, dragonflies have been prevalent throughout history in Japanese literature (mainly haiku) as well as in various art forms. In China, we see the dragonfly associated with prosperity, harmony, and good luck! Amongst the Native Americans, the creature is honoured as a symbol of purity in that it "eats off of the wind itself!"

This creature which is believed to have once been a true dragon, holds deep spiritual meanings for many. The iridescence of this insect's wings, for example, is believed by many to represent the dispersion of illusions and a grand awakening to reality before one's eyes. As iridescence allows your eyes to see changes in colour depending on the angle of the sunlight, so we are given complete view of all changes and what these changes mean in a very transparent sense that does not allow for any illusions or deceit. As a creature of both water and wind (spirit and change), the dragonfly has been deeply engraved into malleability towards life's changes as well as the subconscious mind and one's ability to listen and heed subconscious impressions and prompts. We can now put together a picture of the dragonfly as a catalyst that pulls on the higher realms of spirituality and subconscious while bringing that light down into the lower realms of physical, every day life, thus illuminating the truth in our daily realities— not distracting from it— but actually highlighting the deeper meanings and even the plain meanings that are often overlooked and can only be seen with an elevated ability of foresight. Again, this is alluded to by the iridescence of the dragonfly's wings while indwelling both the wind and the water.

Dragonflies can move swiftly in all six directions; moving at speeds of 45 miles per hour, with 20 times more power in each of it's wing strokes as compared to all other insects. This means that it can hover like a helicopter, fly backwards, forwards, up, down, and to both left and right, all while performing with a mere 30 flaps of the wing per minute (compare that to the mosquito's 600 times a minute and the housefly's 1000 flaps per minute); thus we witness how much effortless grace and exceeding power this beautiful, iridescent creature possesses! In its short lifespan, the dragonfly leaves nothing to be desired! It spends most of its life as a nymph underwater, where it ferociously hunts its prey (including small fish), while only a fraction of its life is spent as an airborne adult! But the fact isn't obvious while observing a dragonfly as it leaps with great joy through the air, and hovers over the surface of the water contemplating the many reflections it sees through its 360 degree eyesight! One would think it would live forever! Unfortunately, the opposite is the case as this flying beauty has only a few months to spare! The dragonfly teaches us, shows us, how to live in the moment, to live life to the fullest and leave nothing to want! It reminds us to fly in all directions, see all reflections, with ease and aplomb. She reminds us of effortless grace, he encourages us to hover and draw from the soul, gaining the vision to defeat illusions, deceit, and see clearly into reality. She calls us to accompany her and we, too, can skitter over the surface of our existence and examine it from the perspective of different dimensions. This is not exemplified only in the dragonfly's movements over the water, but also more blatantly in the fact that almost 80% of this insect's brainpower is dedicated to its eyesight! And that eyesight being, as I mentioned earlier, a 360 degree view! We are encouraged to see a single thing from a vast array of dimensions, to infiltrate reality with unmasked perspectives, and ultimately, to see ourselves in the light of total absence of fabrications and pretensions, whether they are our own doings, or the result of impressions left by other people.

As you read the writings in this book, I'm sure you will notice that the majority of these poems are remarkably different in comparison to the poetry which can be found in my other books *The Sun Is Snowing* and *The Suns Snow And The Sands Move*. There is a reason for that. While writing the poems contained within this book, I wrote under the influence of the title *All Things Dance Like Dragonflies* and with each stroke of my pen, I truly felt an "emergence" of some sort. A feeling of splendor, as though I had shed a certain skin and was happy to bask under the light in my new form! You will find the writings herein to be more tangible. Yes, *tangible* is the word!

As if seeing the whole entire world through the wings of a dragonfly!

Research resources:

"The Meaning of a Dragonfly: What Does a Dragonfly Symbolize?" Dragonfly-site.com. Accessed 15 Nov. 2012.

"The Hidden or Implied Meaning of Chinese Charm Symbols." Primaltrek.com. Accessed 15 Nov. 2012.

"Dragonfly." Wikipedia, the free encyclopedia. Accessed 15 Nov. 2012.

Molecules

You know the glances
Between the two of us

It could be the most insignificant moments
Like me leaning on the door with a cigarette

And you standing by the window
Looking at me

Creating a recognition
Something– like we are capturing

The same colors in the black and white air
And feeling the same weight of molecules

Molecules float in the air
And they can be anything for us

They can look like anything, for us!
They can be any color

They can mean anything
In between the two of us

The way my cigarette smoke curls
In the air; in my peripheral vision

Can spell out a love letter
On the naked wind

Just because we want it to
If that's what we want it to mean

We can write love letters to each other
In this moment right here

An insignificant moment
But we can master the molecules

We can sail the few feet in between us
On golden ships that we both share

Lies

The silk strings
Are spun by tongues
And tied with fingers

Dark like the black widow
Yet beautiful like
The belief in ten promises

They can dance into each other,
Weave themselves
Into an opalescent web

All that's needed is one breath
A single whisper into the air
They come to life

The strings of silk
The lies they
Settle in the winds

Dirty

If I were completely confident
You would miss out

On my self-chastising
Downward glances

The shy gestures
The way I tug at the ends of my hair

And dance my eyelids around
When you look at my face

And if I had never made mistakes
You wouldn't now see

The willful spark in my eyes
The wise countenance

You wouldn't get to see
What's in my garbage bin

There would be no bin
There would be nothing to know!

C. JoyBell C.

If I were completely void of mischief
You would miss out

On my dirty, unspoken thoughts
That you figure out on the subway

When you sit across from me
And I look into your eyes

You enjoy those thoughts of mine!

Ice Sculpture

Yes that's you
You were never a sorry soul

In fact you have always been
The most beautiful one

That really is you!
You never looked broken!

In fact your cheeks have always caught
The sunlight at a peachy angle

Useless, it was all so useless
The fear, the unbelief in yourself

You wasted time
Being a beggar in your mind

While you were a Queen
All the while! All along!

Don't talk to me about brokenness
You were never meant to see yourself

That way

C. JoyBell C.

You were always meant to see
The masterpiece that you are!

Don't talk to me about inadequacy
You have always been the swan

The Swan, The Eagle, The Pegasus

The ice sculpture
That refused to melt!

The only inadequacy of you
Were the thoughts you had about you!

Stand in the noontime sun, ice sculpture!
Look at how you frost and glisten!

Unafraid and beautiful
It's always been this way

Strength and Honesty

If I told you that I didn't need you
Or anyone,

That would be a lie
I know it

I need you
I need lots of things!

And if I told you that I
Don't belong to anyone

That would be me afraid
I want to belong to you

You should belong to me, too
I want you to!

If I were to tell you that
I never made mistakes

That would be me pretending.
I've made mistakes, I think!

I have a trash can you can look through

C. JoyBell C.

I'm not empty

If I said I wasn't lost, not ever
That wouldn't be the truth

I'm often lost and because
I can see that, I know that

I'm really alive! And living!
I can get lost, too!

But you, you can find me!
I don't need to lose myself

In you

She Who Still Dreams

I see a woman with dreams
Her head is held high,
her gaze straightforward.
She is petite
But
In all of her littleness
She raises herself up towards the sky
And occupies
All of herself that there is to be!
Her gestures are sure
Her stride; nothing special
but it is her own! Her own
walk into the world every day!

That's how I know she has dreams.

That's how I know she still dreams.

The Woman In The Sunlight

Today I watched a woman walk beneath the sun's rays
I watched her for a few seconds
The strands of hair on her head illuminated under the
noontime sun like Swarovski under a bulb
The deep lines around her mouth introduced me to
Her former youth, her wedding day, the birth of her first
child (and the second and the third)
The engraved creases in her dark olive skin told me a story
of her many laughters, happy moments
I watched small shadows sneak their way underneath
strands of her wind-rustled bangs
The evident lines on her forehead welcomed me into her
home and
I heard her crying that day when he left her; I saw her
sorrow the time she thought she was forgotten!
The wind blew sunlight over her face, pushing aside
invisible curtains so I
Could see herself emerge as she strode down the lane;
The woman's bone structure looked emulsified in
determination and confidence
A face molded, sculpted by the hands of Memory and
Venture
Sort of a satisfying sensation tingled over my skin
Ah, to smell all the scents of a beautiful soul exhaled to me
in the wind!

Myself

I trust this woman
She can go home
And go places
And do everything she wants to do,
have everything she wants to have!
This is someone I trust
Because she can.
Nothing can get in her way
She can laugh whenever she wants to laugh,
she can laugh loud when she wants to!
She can take on the world! Because it's her
Oyster
And I trust her
Because she can
Because she is

This woman, this portrait of me.

I Couldn't See

I looked at myself
In the mirror
Dim
Shadowy
My eyelids dropped
In shame
Of my reflection

Flawed skin
Odd shape
Silly-looking stare

And I mourned my reflection
I travailed
My heart turned in dismay
Of the erred
The insufficient
The lack
The flaws

Many days passed
Months
Years

He bought me a light
Tall and bright

He stood it beside my mirror
"Here" he said
The light was bright
Too bright
It hurt my eyes

First there was fear
The unknown...
What might it be...

I turned the light off, stepped away.
But today I approached my mirror,
Turned on my bright new light,
At first it hurt my eyes and
I anticipated shame; But!
In the absence of the shadowy dimness

All flaws disappeared
My skin shone and proudly framed
My beautiful shape!

My stare wasn't silly; but
In the brightness of the light
My eyes beat with their own heartbeats!
In my face
There is a promise, a forthright beauty
Nothing to be ashamed of

C. JoyBell C.

Everything to be proud of

It was never that way, at all!
I was always beautiful!
I just couldn't see it!

Venus

An apple tree planted in an orange grove will
Still bear apples
A swan born in the ducks' haven will
Still become beautiful
An eagle fallen into the cave of bats will
One day gain its sight

When God plants a blue rose
Red paint will wash away

Venus born to a man and a woman
Will still be risen by God, from the foam of Liguria

Feathers

It will be okay
When you return to you
To the you who
Was there
Before the floods came
Before the castle toppled down
Before the earth shook, quaked

It will be okay
It will be silent
Serene
When you find yourself standing there
In the same place where you left
You

When you wonder if it's okay
To go and take your hand
To touch your face
And look into your eyes again
And find you,

You will see

That you have found

The place where feathers rain
And the Qilin tramples
Not even a single
Blade of grass

And your heart
Breaks not
Does not crack

Go back. It's okay.

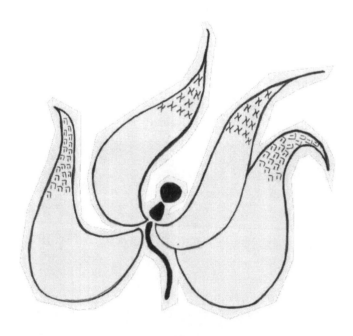

C. JoyBell C.

Who Is She?

Who is this?
who has given me her irises
Takes me by the hand
And shows me where
The vision of me still stands:
In the place of feathers
Where the Qilin roams
Washed in the light
Of all the suns and all the moons
Me standing there
Who is this: she leads me back and forward
And stands with me before my mirror—
Through whose eyes I see
Myself
Clothed in beauty
Emancipated by beauty
She is beauty

I am beauty

Daughter of Zeus

At the feet of Zeus on Oros Olympos
Stood a single blue rose

"Why do you cry, blue rose?" asked Zeus.
"Because I am not made of nature!" said blue rose.
"Why do you bleed, blue rose?" asked Zeus.
"Because they value what is made of nature more than
what is not!" said the blue rose.
"Blue rose, do you not know, that what is not made by
nature, is made by the hands of the gods? Blue rose, do
you not know, that what does not exist in nature, *is* the
blood of the gods? And do you not know that splendor is
not found in numbers? Is a field of daisies more eminent
than a single blue rose?" her father Zeus answered.

"But they don't understand!"

"We do not exist to be understood; we exist because
we are."

Dear Son

And every day I become
The intricate details upon
The lace that is your life
Your voice mingles in the melodies of mine
You fill the space that is beside me
And I the space that is beside you
Yet always, I find myself striving
Aiming to weave my joys into the pattern of
Your lace even more so.
So that I may dance with you
And you may dance with me too

My Friend

Yes, it was me who was with you in your dream
Last night, I dreamt it too!
There we sat in the room on top of the world
And we watched her destroy herself
Bombs, explosions, warring, battling
You told me of a great writer's words
The words you taught me stay with me today
You told me of a new discovery of yourself
Now I see you evermore, clearly,
To know you truly, in my dreams at night
You, my friend
I know who you are

C. JoyBell C.

I Want To Live

I feel as though I wish to explode! For if I am able to
explode, all the tiny particles of me would scatter into
all directions and end up everywhere you could possibly
imagine and I imagine that maybe I would truly live
because I would then be able to feel myself in
everywhere and in everything and I myself would be
able to feel everywhere and everything, all at the same
time and like never before! And each tiny particle of me
would be breathing all in unison, so I would be
breathing a trillion breaths all at once!
When I think about that, I can feel how much I want it.
I want to live.

Animalistic

The veins in his arms
Protruded right below the
Very surface of his skin
And a faint hue of scarlet
Spread itself slowly
His flesh washed in warmth
And bound by his skin
Were shapely muscles
Tense and firm
I detected beads of sweat
Appear on his brow
Right along his hairline

The movement of your blood through your veins
The pulsating throb of your heart in your chest
The distributing warmth running through your flesh

It grabs me
It pulls me

And I can feel my own pulse beat faster
As if my own arteries share in your blood
I can feel my forehead moisten with sweat
You'd think we were covered in the same skin

C. JoyBell C.

It was a humid summer afternoon
The day he walked into that place
I like to watch the heat of the sun
Work its wonders on
A red-blooded man

Release

I let it go
I let it go
I let it go
I let it go
I let it go

All of it

My Son,

I want to wrap up this world
Then throw it into the trash
And make a new world for you

I want to tie up the lies, the deception
Bind up the threats, the hurt
Crumple it all and throw it away,

Give you a new world.
I want to make a new world for you
And make it a wonderful world!

If I could roll it all up
And cast it all away
I would, For you

If I could form a new ocean
A new mountain
A new valley, a new horizon

I would, For you

So I write to the people
Setting them free
One day, your world will be

Free

So I talk to the people
I give them wings
One day, your world will be

Winged

So I call to the people
I give them gifts
One day your world will be

Beautiful

So I pull down principalities
Expose their hiding places
One day your world will be

Light

My son,

I can't wrap up this world
And birth a new one for you
So I will change this one

So one day you will have
Only beauty and sight and freedom

C. JoyBell C.

Only trust and courage and light

Because I love you my son
I will change this world
For you

How Great Is This Love?

How great is this love of mine?
That I would swallow up worlds
For you?

How great is this love?
I would conceive, again and again,
New worlds for you!

The only thing that can change
This universe is
My love for you

I will place wings upon horses
I will place wings upon stones
I will plant roses in the rocks

For you

Because you walk this earth
I will remake it for you
I will reanimate

Remove, recreate
Rebirth, reform, I will
Cast in stone and write in sand

C. JoyBell C.

To keep, To wash away

Because your feet walk this earth,
It must be a new earth!
It must be an earth of streams

Roses, swans, and love
Life, courage, strength
Freedom, belief, beauty

It will not be as it is now
It will not stay this way
I will remake the earth

A new life
I will breathe into it
Living things will come forth

Your world, My gift to you

How great is this love, my son?

Bigger Than The Worlds

They say (to their children)
I will give you this gold

They say (to their children)
I will give you this house

They say (to their children)
I will give you this vineyard

They tell them (their children)
I will give you this land

This throne, this island
This name, this history

But I tell you
I will birth a new world
For you

I tell you
I will create a new world

For you

C. JoyBell C.

I say to you
Any world is yours

Because I love you
My son

Alive!

The world!
It skips and leaps with life!

The frog on my windowsill
Two frogs, actually…

The raindrops breathe
And scream as they hit the ground!

Rain creates streams
That flow like life force

Through my garden
Dripping down the hole in the ground

The world!
It is full and bursts with life!

There is a bee
Flying around my tea!

But I really like lightning bugs
And dragonflies

There are beings
Whispering into my ear unseen

The breaths of
Unseen faces

Playing with each other
Skipping with each other

What I see
And what I can't see

All alive

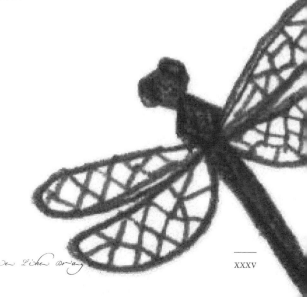

All Things Wander Like Away

You Need To Know

You have to know
What angels look like

What gods smells like
And what demi-gods sound like

You have to know
Where they emerge

Hear their wings unfold
Recognize the stare in their eyes

What their skin feels like
You have to taste

You have to know

Because if not

Life to you will become
A blind date

A walk through the park
With no eyes, no skin

C. JoyBell C.

No sight No feeling
Yes you'll see the ordinary

But how extraordinary
Would it be

If you knew an angel
When you met one?

If you knew a goddess
When you met one?

It's like you're digging
And find a diamond

You sell the diamond for a cent
Because you don't know what it is

It's like you're digging
And find a diamond

Using it in a fire
Because you think it's a coal

Angels need to be seen

Crazy

Of course I want to escape
Onto your branches
And fondle the roots
Play hide and seek
The Dark Hedges
Send messages to me
Sprayed onto the morning mists
And as the day breaks
Every morning
I fling myself
Like a crazy soul
From tree to tree
Branch to branch
Every swing is wild
Unanticipated
The spirits are large
Some are white and some are dark
They jump with me
I overcome them all
From tree to tree like a crazed soul
With desires divine and atrocious
These trees two hundred years old
Or more?
The Dark Hedges
On Bregagh Road

C. JoyBell C.

And I fling myself
Into an insane frolicsome happiness
I'm made of the same stuff
That this bark and these roots
Are made of
I am
Daughter of the forest
Element of the trees
I cast my shadow
To the wind
And color my soul
With the moon!

800 Pages

Did you know that while I was looking at you
I tried to pull you inside of me
Compelling you to look up
From your thick book
Probably 800 pages

I'd never seen an angel like you before, your
Black leather and metal spikes
Made your thin, peach skin
Look like alabaster
An angel

Did you know I like torn jeans? I liked yours!
And the big messy hair; it
Didn't scare me at all
Do you always hide
Behind your hair?

You're a different kind of angel, because you
Hide beneath black and thorns
Your golden hair is messy
But your skin glows
Beneath it all

C. JoyBell C.

I wanted to make you look up from your book
So I pulled your soul into mine
But you were too shy
So you hid yourself
Behind your book

I wanted you to come home with me, angel
And that day on the subway
You sitting there
In front of me
I wanted

To touch you

To make you mine

To make it all okay

Why do you hide yourself, angel? Are you afraid
Of them? They can't hurt you!
Bright angel of golden light
Don't hide behind black
And sharp thorns!

Let me take you into me and keep you safe
Look up! Angel in the subway!
Just one look is all it takes
I'll make everything okay

Come home with me

The Beloved

She holds the small one in her arms
Cradling her, calling out her name
The small, beautiful one is highlighted
Under the magnanimous rays of the sun
Her hair is chocolate-colored and golden-red
The small one
A beauty that stills time,
Causes the air to be still around her

The small one smiles

And I think

She does not deserve pain
She will not be deserving of fear,
Of envy, She will never deserve to
Be disappointed, to cry, to be afraid
All of the darkness around her
Should never go near her
The beloved, the favored one
A deific being born in
The valley of titans and traitors

Please

Protect her

Don't let her fall, don't let her cry
Don't let them hurt her
Many a day she has still to come
A whole, beautiful life awaits her
Please hold her, please don't leave her
Don't turn your back on her

The small one, the beautiful one

The Stray

She looked weary and worn
Her stomach bloated
Having just given birth

She lay in the rock garden
Over summer-roasted stones
Calmly contemplating

I sat down at the glass doors
And slowly opened them
So to not give her a fright

I coocd and called out to her
Cautiously she heeded my voice
And doubtingly made her way t'wards me

Two slices of bologna I tore
And fed to her piece by piece
She glanced up at me

With her big, green eyes
Every time she came near to take a bite
So afraid was she

Yet through all her fear
Through all her doubt

She remained graceful

She was of lowly status
Perchance this was her biggest meal
The most food she had ever seen!

Four slices of bologna
Two small fish and some cheese
A shallow cup full of cold water, too

In all her lowliness
In all her lack of glory
She held her head high, gracefully

She moved with the flow of honor
And dignity; I called her into my home
But she wouldn't dare put her paws on my floor!

She looked at my floor, then she looked at herself
And thought herself not worthy to step inside!
But still, she held her head high!

Grace and dignity clothed her
From the tip of her tail to her paws
Her big green eyes so beautiful

She ate until she could eat no more!

C. JoyBell C.

Her kittens called to her from behind the fountain
Her face so small, expressed so much gratitude!

The cat did not think herself of great stature
She did not see herself to be of so much worth
But she knew grace and dignity

But she knew gratitude

Oh all the people who ought to be like this cat...

The Cat Is A Whore

There once was a stray cat
Who visited me and showed
Me humility and grace

The stray visited me again
Today and along with her
She brought two tomcats

I realize that the stray cat
Is a whore; impregnated over
And over again by her toms

In her eyes, she knows her
Lowly state, and from life
She expects nothing more

But a small morsel of food is
All she asks to fill her heart
With joy! She asks for no

Carpet to sleep on, for no
Roof over her head, she
Doesn't even expect to

Be seen as anything more
Than a whore! Oh this
Stray cat, in all her humility

Is adorned with such grace
When God looks at her
He does not look at her in hate

The stray cat that is covered
In grace and clothed in
Humility, her heart which

Covers a multitude of sins

To Be Free

You tire me with your
Complaints and dreams
With your travails and woes

Here we are, together
Together in the same cage
Shut up and stop ranting in my ear!

As if I care!

Night and day, I look out
Of this cage and close my eyes
In my mind's eye I can feel

How the free wind feels on my face
How it feels to go with the river
To run with the equines

To be free

How Can I Still Smile?

I look at you and see the
Shadows of our cage bars
Align across your face

We share a cage together
Day after day, I have to watch
The shadows of our cage door

Rise on your face with the sunrise
And slowly fall with the sunset
Reminding me that I am not free

How can I still smile, when I look at you?

Far Away

But! I will escape in my dreams at night!
And in my fantasies during the day!
I will soar, I will fly
Swirling up with paints of red
Paints of blue, yellow, purple, green!
I will flow with the colours and wash over
The canvas that is this world
The canvas that is this day
And tomorrow and yesterday

And these paints will form the images
Of the stars in the sky, the flowers in the field!

These paints will form the images
Of the water in that river, the swan on that brook!

These paints will form the images
Of the tears on your face, the gleam in your eyes

These paints will form the images
Of the birds of paradise, the equines on the shoreline!

You will see your soul on this canvas
This canvas that is me! This paper that is me!

This sky that is me! This sea that is my soul!
You will see me in everything, I will be there
Because I will escape in my dreams at night
And in my fantasies during the day! I will
Not stay here, imprisoned, afraid! Things may never
Change and it may always be this way but
I promise that you will see me in the dawn and
In the dusk, you will feel me in the noontime sun
And bask in my glow under the moon! I will touch

Your skin with raindrops and sing to you on the winds!
You will feel me; you will know me, in everything!

I will be there, because I will run far away from here!

Flama Eterna

It was a suddenly lit wick
Burst of a single flame

Right here in the middle of my chest
Here— right here in the heart of my soul!

It felt like nothing I have ever felt before
There's never been a wick lit in me before

And for no reason
Sitting at the dinner table

Unassuming was I
The benefactor of a new pilot light!

A newly lit candle
Gently it exploded into flame

I felt it here— in the middle of my chest
Right here in the heart of my soul!

I have had many new beginnings before
But never a candlewick lit!

C. JoyBell C.

I hadn't even known that there
Was a candle residing within me

All along!

Until it lit

And I smiled a glowing smile!

Because in that moment I knew
That it is never-ending!

In that very moment I understood
That this flame will never go out!

It Is Time To Be Loved

Why do you feel such a need to be
Loved by the people you were born to?

To be cherished by those who raised you?
To be admonished by those who share your blood?

God has given you the whole world
The whole world loves you!

You still climb the stairs on your knees
To get to the top of the tower!

Why do you still sojourn in the darkness?
As the leaves fall to the ground dead

And the bats flutter, the cold wind bites!

You still traverse; you go to their homes!
To knock at their doors! To be seen!

To be loved

Why do you need so much to be
Loved by those useless pigs?

C. JoyBell C.

They sit around their table and drink
They feed their faces with lard

They dine on skunk meat
Skunk on golden plates

Why do you still sit and wait
For them to call your name?

Please stop!

Your knees are bleeding!
Your hands are cold and chaffed!

Please stop!

Your skin is torn by the winds!
Your heart troubled by the bats!

Please stop!

Child of the sun!
Daughter of Zeus!

They were but instruments of your birth!
They were but birds who built your nest!

Fly now!

Your were born of the Gods
Given to the world

Leave the blind pigs!
May they succumb to vampires!

The love in your heart
Is sweeter than honey

The eyes that cherish you are eyes
That the world is not worthy to behold!

The eyes of the Gods watch you
The elves and the sirens pray for you!

Leave the lonely tower behind!
Forsake the godless tribe!

Desert the god-forsaken walls!
Forget those made of clay and mud!

You are made of air, water, and fire!
Their blood you never shared!

C. JoyBell C.

Welcome, beloved of the Gods!
Welcome into the chamber of your Father!

Welcome, child of the Heavens!
Welcome to the whole wide world!

It is time to abandon
It is time *to be loved*

In The Present Moment

Oh the satisfaction endowed
By living in the present moment!
It is like a deep, replenishing gulp
Of living waters! Or your favorite soda!

Oh how the heart beats stronger
Every beat an assurance of existence
A reminder of the present, a promise
Of a foreseen future in beauty and grace

Oh how the strange birds' sounds
Become suddenly so much louder
When my mind is right here, right now
In steady unison with my heartbeat!

Oh how a simple small smile
Feels like so much more on the inside
When I have no thoughts of useless things
Like what other people need to think of me

Oh how the door to my future is filled
With genuine intensity of light and love
When I take no interest in proving things
To people who don't even deserve it

C. JoyBell C.

Oh how true happiness comes to be
When I take interest in actually being happy!
With no thought of making other people know
About my being happy!

Oh how sweet life is!
When it is lived in the moment!
Life lived for no one else but myself!
Myself and those few whom I love, who love me!

It's Okay

I forgive you because
I can't blame you for
All that you couldn't be

I forgive you because
I can't blame you for
Not being all that I wanted

I forgive you because
Who am I to say
That it could have been better?

Who am I to say that
You could have given more?
When that is you

And I am me

You have your own story

And I have mine

You have your own reasons
You have your own pain
You have your own sorrow

You fell over a tree stump
I fell over an ant hill

You were bitten by the bees
I was bitten by the wasps

You smiled because there was a cake
I smiled because there was soda pop

You laughed because the moon danced
I laughed because those stars sang

That is you
This is me

You don't have to be
Good enough for me

You only have to be
Good enough for yourself

I forgive you
Please forgive me too

For wanting what you couldn't be
I love you for all that you can be

For all that you are

Forgive You

I smile because
I have forgiven you

If I need to I
Will forgive you

Again and again
Again and again

And
Again

Birth Of A Star

A flame was lit
Upon a candlewick
That was placed in my heart

Last night the flame

Gave birth to a star

Dancing Dragonflies

If you hadn't fallen into the hole
Lost your way, fallen
Into the darkness of that abyss
If you were not secluded in destitution
Left to grasp and grope for
Anything that your hands could touch
If you were not thrown into lamentation
Bereavement, lack, loss, need

You would have never known that
There was something out there
For you
That there was something else

For you
That there was the golden hand
That statue standing in the dark
The angel reaching out to you
It was always there, but you never knew
You never saw it, any of it
Until the light was lost
Until you couldn't see anything!

Funny how the most important things
The stuff of destiny and magic
Can only first come into recognition
When the light has departed

In the darkness, you reached out as far
As you could reach, grasped for anything
Your fingers could graze!
You cried out in the blackness
For something, for something
You reached, you grasped,
You strived to find
And so you found!

You found all the things you would
Have never seen, never believed in
Had the lights not gone out!
Had you not fallen to your lowest!

In the depravity you found
The angel's golden hand
In the emptiness you found
Old maps you had forgotten
Upon the walls of the abandoned cave
You felt the handwritings of God
And deciphered His hidden messages
Written by His own finger there *for you*

When you fell onto the ground and
Their feet walked on top of you
It's down there in the mud where you
Were lifted up by seraphic hands
Nourished by the elementals
Taken in by fawns and satyrs
Fed by elves and sages
Saved by the prayers of old!

Do not mourn the pain, the despair
Do not weep over the fall
If you had not been to the valley of death
You would have never come to find
The secret pathway, the shortcut
To glories untold, to the mirror of your soul!
Oh but the fall— it was the beginning of
The rest of your Destiny!

Oh but the fall— the detour
Brought you to your highest calling!
In the darkness, you found the light
But isn't that where true light is found?
When all light is gone, there is
Some left somewhere
The illuminations that
Never die, which were meant to be!

C. JoyBell C.

The numerous, luminous open windows!
The dancing dragonflies, yours to keep!
The lights, the doors of your *Destiny*!

Sienese Yellow

The sunlight in Siena
Is yellow like no other yellow!
The sunlight in Siena
Is a yellow that lights
The Sienese bricks afire!
And bathes my skin
In golden hues!
The Sienese yellow
Cascades onto my shoulders
Like an awaited wedding veil
Softly, gently casting shadows
That fall around my ankles
Like anklets, like jewellery
Of the gods, like puddles
Of tranquil rain that
Have gathered to rest
At my feet

Silently the shadows cast
Follow me around wherever
In Siena that I may wander!
While the golden tint of
Sienese sunlight defiantly
Cohorts with my body

C. JoyBell C.

Sending my reflection on the windows
Into languishes of ecstasy
Supreme fantasy
In my mind's eye
My reflection dances a hedonistic dance
Tripping and skipping
From one window pane to another
The silhouette of the sun's purpose
Captured in my countenance
Happening in that flicker
Which you can catch in my eyes!

Fireflies

Some lights, like fireflies
Light up in the darkness
They lead the way
And you follow them like
A six-year-old on a
Summer night catching
Lightning bugs

But you would have never,
Ever even seen them
If darkness did not fall
If sun did not depart
If lights did not hide behind
The shadows
When nighttime stole time

Some lights show up
When you look for them
When you try to find them
Then you'll see them
Then you'll feel them
You'll catch them!
In a jar, like fireflies!

C. JoyBell C.

Nobody sees lightning bugs
In the morning
No one catches a firefly at noon
I have never heard of
A lightning bug chase in the dawn!
They are alive in light and darkness
But they glow in the night!

Answers cannot come
When we think we already know them
The truth can't be seen
When we think we already know it
Answers and truth
Come when we look for them!
Curse not the night that has fallen

The darkness has given you many things!

Blue Parade

The marching band has come!
Wearing a blue-hued uniform
That seems to light the air afire
With castings of the same color
Condensing on everything around!

I don't think anyone else has noticed
The otherworldly blue hue
That has washed our vision
And settled us down in a calm
A deep calm, a serenity

This tranquil *cerulean* is a shade
Of the imagination!
Captured by their hats,
Vests, skirts and pants!
An empyrean entity enters with this hue

An open door for the elementals
A bird's call to the nearby Heavens
Like a dance of cyan birds of paradise
The marching band flaunts itself
In this parade, through these streets

C. JoyBell C.

Creating a noise almost unbearable
But soothing the eyes phenomenally!
They twirl their batons
They hammer those lyres
And beat those drums to kingdom come!

But why is it that only you and I
Can see the azure sunset cast
Into the air by this ethereal shade?
We wonder where they bought such cloth!
But does anyone else even notice?

All the others watch the dancing
And hide their ears from the
Horrendous sound!
Not noticing anything different
While we ascend to spiritual places!

Thanks to this shade of blue!

Coloured Souls

Let my eyes peer into the blue-green
Hue of your soul and may that shade
Reflect upon the amethyst surface of
My own heart!

Let me look into the window and see
All the pictures of you lined up on
Your wall
Let me know who you are

I will give you a letter and draw you
Many pictures of all the things that
I want to say but I can't because
I don't know how to say them

You can watch me draw in crayons
And I will imitate my drawings by dancing
And skipping, moving over the ground
In beautiful motions for you

And I can take a lantern to the walls
Of your room and see closely the
Faces of you, captured in film
Hanging loosely on strings

C. JoyBell C.

So I can know you
And you can know me too

Our Shadows

I saw your shadow today
Leaning up against the willow tree
It was blue and danced in the
Mirages of the summer heat
Rising from the surface of the street

You saw my shadow? I saw yours too
When you weren't looking because
You were busy catching dragonflies
And it fluttered like their wings!
Your soul fluttered like airy diamonds!

I watched your blueness stop
And look at me
Then it lifted and swam through the air
It landed in front of me
And sang a song to me

You were so beautiful
You fluttered like transparent wings
You glistened like diamonds
I came to you on the winds and
Your soul scattered like a cloud of dragonflies

I saw us rise
We rose together
I saw us mingle
Like sunlight in dewdrops
We tasted each other

C. JoyBell C.

The Elemental

Have I forgotten what your voices
Sound like?
You spoke to me often while I stood
Under your shadows, watching your
Branches sway in the wind! I knew
All of your voices so well! They were
All at once familiar, something I had
Always known from the beginning
Of time

Have I forgotten the song that you
Sang to me?
I stood at your side and you sang to me
Endlessly
Songs that turned my soul, which embraced
My heart! Songs that only you and I knew!
I knew your song by heart, I recognized you!
You called to me often and I came to you
To stand by your side as you flowed through the city

Have I forgotten the ways that you danced
For me?
I walked into your home and your brightly
Colored skirts skimmed the blades of grass
As you twirled, your petals facing the sunlight
And you opened up for me, you left nothing

For yourselves, you dance with your hearts!
Bright red and immaculate white
You swayed to the echoes of the brook!

How could I have forgotten the sound of
Your voices?
Wake me up again, and cause me to hear
To recognize!
I feel the faint whispers of your tongues
As I once knew them, oh spirits of the trees!
You speak to me in many different voices
You call to me on many varied tongues
Come to me again, take me back in!

How could I have forgotten the words
To your songs?
Flood my soul with your lyrics!
Do not let me wander far!
Overtake my steps and lift me up into
Your waves and ripples! Bathe me in
Your lyrics! Oh great spirit of the waters!
The river, the brook, the lake, the ocean, the sea!
Forgive me for forgetting, take me back to you!

How could I have forgotten the steps that
You taught me?
How could I have let go of
The way your bodies moved

C. JoyBell C.

The steps you taught me to take, the movements
You showed me to dance!
How could the dances have escaped me?
When I walked with you, oh spirit of the rose!
You burst your petals open everywhere I tread!

Spirit of the rose, take me back, come back to me!
Spirits of the great trees of this earth, forgive me!
Heart of the water, forgive me for forgetting!
Forgive me, forgive me, forgive me, take me back in!
I want you, I need you here with me!
I am lost without you, my home! My family!
Do not let me go astray, hold onto me! Keep me!
Talk to me again, sing to me again, dance for me
All over again!

It was the humans— they hurt me too much
They numbed my ears with their
Loud noises of betrayal and jealousy! They cut away
My sense of feeling with their blades of envy!
It was the humans— they enticed me to be as their own
They tempted me to be one of them, to hear
Only their voices!
I trusted them and they betrayed me
They left me for dead!

I am sorry, my family! I am sorry I wandered
I went astray!

But I am the prodigal daughter
Now I have come home, now I hear
Your voices again, you speak to me in the
Voice of the vagabond bird who visits my window
You have found me, you searched for me and
You found me!
You left all the others, to come and look for me!

You sent the bird and you visited me in my dreams
None of you ever left me, you stayed with me
Again and again you spoke, you sang your songs
You danced your dances for me! Even when I
Could not hear, could not feel, could not see!
The bird sang the once familiar song
To the sad one who was me— who could not remember!
Like one stricken with amnesia, not recognizing
Her own lover's voice!

Faithful, loyal, and true are you! All of you!
My true family, my true friends, my home!
In the daytime you called to me in the winds
In the night you were with me in my dreams!
You will avenge my sorrows, my hurts, my pains
You will avenge me, against all those who pulled
Me astray!
You will protect me from the envious, the cruel
The traitors and the tempters!

C. JoyBell C.

And I will never be lost again!

I Don't Want To Be Cinderella

I was told that if I was nice
I would reap rewards

I was nice but then
They stabbed me in the back!

I was told that the more
I gave, I would receive

I gave out all the cookies in my jar
And so I was left with none!

My mother taught me the virtue
Of being like Cinderella

I became like Cinderella
But there was no fairy godmother!

My father taught me the virtue
Of being hard-to-get

I was the hardest to get
The easy ones took what I wanted

So many virtues
All those lessons

What a waste!
What a waste of time!

What a useless pursuit!
Of false righteousness!

The more you keep
The more you have!

The more you attract
The more will come

If they fear you
They will cower

Cinderella needed
A knock over the head!

Over and Over Again and Again

Oh my son! For you
The moon has been swallowed
Over and over again and again!
I swallow it!

I have called the white horses
Of the seas, caused the earth
To tremble and quake
Opened and reopened doors

I have sung a song to the sirens
That have sweetened their hearts
All for you!
Even the sirens do not deceive you!

The sirens and the satyrs,
And the nymphs lift you up!
'Til the ends of the earth and beyond!
Oh my laughter runs wild!

My laughter spins wildly
As I think of all the goodness in store
All the good and the great things
That lay themselves down for you!

C. JoyBell C.

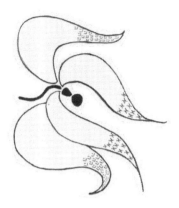

Kein ayin hora!
B'li ayin hara!

Oh my son! For you
This planet and even more
They are not too much to give!
The moons I have swallowed

Over and over again and again

All Things Dance Like Dragonflies

At The End Of The Journey

When you return to glory
To the Heavens of the Universe
To your home among the stars
To your form in the constellations

How will it feel?

Will it feel like victory at the end
Of a battle? Like a triumphant roar?
Is it going to feel like finally waking
From a bad dream? Eyes opened...

Is that how it is going to feel?

I think it will feel like just another day
Because though you walk the earth now
Your spirit bears the stars that belong to you
Your imprint is of the gods, the God, the goddesses

It will be just another day

Another day in your eternity
You swim in your eternity; every day
Is just a fleeting moment, a joy or a hardship
A happiness or a struggle; but at the end of the day

You are bound to God hand and foot

C. JoyBell C.

At the end of the day, you return in your dreams
You escape this deafening stupor
And swim to the ends of the earth, jumping off
Back into where you came from!

After all of this, it will be your day

Your day of birth back into your nature
Your homecoming, when all of *that* will feel
Like merely one day in your eternity and you
Will look below at what has passed, as if you always knew

The question is: will you choose to journey again?

Thunder Storm

I call to you, lighting!
Give me your power!

I call to you, grey skies!
Give me your beauty!

I call to you winds!
Whisper to me secrets!

I am filled to the brim

Caim

My love
With your finger
Cast a *caim* on me
Move your finger
Along the outline
Of my skin
Just near enough
To feel my body warmth
Just far enough
To hover like a halo
Turn with the sun
Clockwise from the ground
Raise your incantation
Up from my feet
And all around me
Surround me, my love
Draw a halo all around me
Protection near
And danger afar
Light near
And darkness afar
Keep peace within
Keep evil without
Keep hope within
Keep doubt without
Here while we stand
Under the moon by the waves
On this cliff
Or if you want

I can lay on the shore
You can draw the *caim* around me
In the sea's sands
I can cast one over you, too
I will be within your God's protection
And you will be within mine

My love
You have made me an angel

Caim

(n.) Gaelic: lit. "sanctuary", "encircling", "protection"; is a form of
ancient Celtic prayer practiced amongst the early Celtic
Christians, and is still valid unto this day. The circle of protection
is drawn around the person in the air with one's finger, whilst
saying the caim prayer. The act of this ritual is called "casting a
caim."

C. JoyBell C.

Saudade

You're gone but
The remnant of how your hair smells
And your nonchalant stride
How your eyes squint in the morning sun
The way you smile at me between coffee
And egg muffins
Absent-minded looks of love
In the dizzy, trance-like state of waking
Too early in the morning
All of that is stuck onto me
Like dispersed honeycomb
At the bottom of the honey bottle
It won't come off
Like orange pulp
On the sides of my orange juice box
Irritatingly clingy
Impossible to take off
You're never coming back

But the pieces of you
Still stick to me
They're blown onto the surface of me
Like autumn leaves in the wind
Like the million pieces of a love letter torn apart
They keep on reappearing with the winds
And those winds smell like you
The air smells like everywhere we've been together
Sounds like everything we did together
Feels like the dreams that we made

Together
Reminds me of the way your hand feels
How your fingers feel in between mine
You're never coming back

But does that even matter?
When a million pieces of you
Are scattered all over inside me?

saudade

(n.) Portuguese word pertaining to "the love that remains" after
losing someone you love. Echoes the longing, the yearning, a
deeply emotional nostalgia; the continuity of love with a person
you once had or a time that you once lived in.

C. JoyBell C.

Hoppipolla

You know
I still remember the way your perfume smelled
You jumped up and down
The muddy water in the puddle
Splashed
Some mud even landed on my chin
Your hair bounced
And froze in the summer wind
All around your face
Rose petals
The air always smelled like
Rose petals
When we jumped
And skipped around
In those muddy puddles
Your eyes would twinkle
You know?
They would twinkle and inside them
I could see myself
You are
My best friend

hoppípolla

(v.) Icelandic word which translates in English to the exact phrase
"jumping into puddles."

Seeds

The mango seed
Unfound and unwanted
Underneath the swaying willow branches
Caught my eye like a joke catches that hidden laugh

Right beneath the surface of the throat!

It was fun
To drive the mango seed
Into the rocky driveway, into the trodden dirt
Pushing it in with my foot, it felt like a small, fun deed

Like how I used to throw seeds all around!

The seed is
A tree now! A little tree sprouting
From the rocky pavement, crawling out from
Beneath the rocks; two days later and it is proud, vibrant

Beautiful, long leaves hopeful and new!

Every seed I touch…

C. JoyBell C.

Chet

Come with me, take my hand
I will show you the vineyards
And forests
Sprung up from my palms
No, they don't grow out of my hands
But it is the palms of my hands that gave them life!
Daughters of the fruits that I ate
It was child's play
Throwing their seeds onto the ground
Later to discover a vineyard!
Sons of the fruits that I dined on
It was child's play
Casting their seeds onto the soil
Later to wake to a garden
The vines entwine and curl
Like ocean waves, like cumulus clouds
And there are the trees!
They reach up high towards the
Transcendence of God
It was child's play
I threw some seeds out the window
One day

Chet

(Chet is the 8'Th letter in the Hebrew alphabet, and is the
embodiment of "life.")

Before The End

The sunlight has reopened
Many a door for me

Look at it emerging
Pushing the doors open

Asking us to come in (or step out)
Telling us there is something more!

We think something is over
But then the sun opens doors

The light calls us beyond
Shows us something more

Before you say "the end"
Consider the sunshine first

Illuminating
Calling

Beckoning
Creating

There is something more

C. JoyBell C.

Ana Beko'ach

You have settled onto me
And into the marrow of my bones
Soft like the infiltration
Of newborn sun on a silent day

You swim inside my veins
Floating as the leaves do
The leaves that fall in autumn
In my mind, they are suspended in mid-air

You are the balm of Gilead
Moistening my ligaments, penetrating my skin
Bringing life eternal
From the realms of Everlasting

Archangels have come
They are bound to me by golden chains
The right hand of God has reached down
He has untangled the strings of my destiny

Oh Ana, Ana Beko'ach
The whisper on ancient lips
The breath of sages and Rabbis
You are sewn into my soul

Float

Sometimes
All that's needed
Is that I
Lift my hands from it
And let it float on the waters
As leaves, petals, boats do
Let it float to the skies
As lanterns and balloons do
So *they*
Can come and take it for me
Make good of my wishes
Whether these desires be for judgment,
Vengeance or even my own joys!
They will come and make good
Of my heart's desires
So long as I lift my hands from it
And let it float

Just Some Purple, Just Some Wishes

I thought I was meant for a unicorn
But I was given the tiger
I thought I was meant to seek refuge
But He put a sword in my hand!
I wanted dreams silent like lace
Soft like velvet
Instead, I stand on the top of the cosmos
I take the moons into my hands
The moons align for me
Instead, I lead an army!
The soles of my feet touch the rocky shore
And as I pass, new life is given to the
Army of stone!

I didn't want to be so much
Didn't want to be seen so much
Nobody wants the need to be brave!
But here in my hand was placed a sword!
Here in my arms is given to me a tiger!
In my soul beats the heart of a thousand cosmic stars
The fabric of my being not made of lace; but of silk!
The physics of my mind built of diamond; not of petals!
The reflection I saw in the mirror
Was one who didn't ask for much
Just some purple and some wishes…
But to me is given this throne
This scepter and this crown!

Inside me breathes a tiger

Now

I am ready
To walk into my new dawn
Beyond the entrance of this door
I am ready to take the first step
Is it my first step?
Or is it really my last step?
Because I feel that I have traversed
Through fire, through brimstone
Through the aerial territory of demons!

Now I am here

This should be my last step
I never want to look back
I want to leave it all behind
I chant endlessly, the prayers and incantations
Of one who longs with the longing
Of two hundred abandoned ships!
I call out like one alone in the forest
I call out with hope
Only to receive no answers!

Now I am here

I am ready
For this to be the last step
And the first step
I am ready for this to be the entrance
To my destiny! I am ready I am ready I am ready
Right now, right here, just this way

Just like this, I am ready
To be taken away
And flung head-first into the beauty

Right here, right now

Fling me head-first into the reality of my
New tomorrow! Join me with the hands
Of those who will journey with me, and catapult us!
Throw us beautifully and perfectly into our dreams
Into our visions, into the future that awaits us there
It is just there beyond this window
Pick me up and hurtle me!
Pick us up, and push us high!
We will never look back, we will never return!

It is now time

C. JoyBell C.

The Finger of God

And God's finger on this canvas
Is the oxygen flowing through this earth
We can see the strokes of oil paints
In the way the wind lifts up our hair
How He lifts up the leaves
Sweeping the seeds of the ground into the air
With a single stroke of His finger
And our hair sweeps over our faces,
Above our heads, entangling itself with the
Mists and the dragonflies
The twigs and the butterflies
The smell of soil and city smog

Alessandra

At first
She didn't even know
How to drink from a saucer!
Drink from a saucer?
Yes, drink from a saucer!
You see, she is a cat! A stray one.
She is so used to drinking from
The ground, eating from the ground
Now when I give her milk on a saucer
She hesitates
But I coax her and slowly she laps
Though at first she was frightened
So I had to pour the milk on the ground
In the beginning she was shy
Afraid to even come near me
I opened the door; she backed away
Thinking to herself that she wasn't good enough
Today she tried to come in, wanted to follow me
After lapping at the milk in the saucer
Over the past months
I have learned things from Alessandra
From that first day, up to today
I've found a friend in a stray whore
Who is always pregnant and with young
She judges no one but herself
Never overestimates her own honor
Taking a long time to trust
Now she's come around
And so have I

C. JoyBell C.

The Lullaby

In her darkest hours
They visit her

They consume all the bit of space
Between her and the material world

In the silhouette
That outlines her body

Within the breath-distance of her skin's warmth
And the rest of the world

Therein scurry the voices of them all
They smell like cinnamon and things almost forgotten

They feel like lamb wool
Like the softest blanket

Not a single inch of her skin is untouched
But they enthrone her in affection

The image of her past touches her shoulder
Whispers in her ear saying she has come so far

The image of her future
Touches her face, tells her she's almost there

Time, angel, and elemental
Whisk her off to her dreams

She falls into a sleep smooth as velvet
Lulled, soothed, comforted

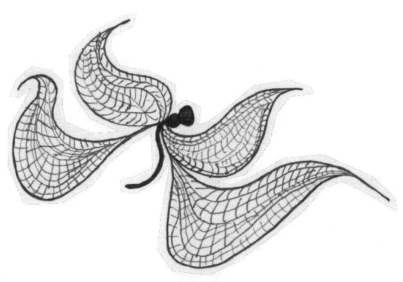

C. JoyBell C.

Roots

The minute she was born into this world
Her soul was rooted into her path of destiny
Looking unto the rainbow that cast itself
Ever so gracefully over her horizon
She looked into her destiny with eyes
Free of defilement and hurt
The path was straight, the rainbow was
Painted vibrantly onto the air
There was no way she would get lost
She stood at the beginning of her own tomorrow
Her soul peered through her path
Her eyes fixated onto her destination
It was grand and good, molded by God's hands

The minute she stepped into church
She was taught to see sin
This was the sin of others
That was the sin of those people
These were the sins of her neighbors
Herself, her family, her friends…
The preacher taught her repentance
The priest taught her to identify insufficiency
On her path where she stood, her gaze
Began to falter as she turned to face the left
And the right: seeking for the sins in others
She began to point, she began to scorn
She began to take offense in actions that did her no wrong

The minute she lost focus of her beautiful rainbow

Her horizon was out of sight
She strayed to the left, she strayed to the right
In pursuit of all that was wrong with the world
All that was wrong with all the people in it
Her vision was no longer set on what was her own
But was set on the shortcomings that were not her own
With these judgments, she filled the void that was inside
The great ravine dug by the hands of her many judgments
The many catechisms tempted her astray
They say sin is temptation
But no greater a temptation is there that exists
Than one's own attraction to self-righteousness

The hands of judgments covered her eyes
The songs of insecurities lulled her intoxicated
She drank on wines of wrath and spite
It was her own pursuit of holiness that
Turned her into a whore; a squanderer of ignorance
She desecrated her own mind
With her judgments of others
The shit in her mind fouled not the people
But only trashed her own spirit!
Until she found herself standing
In the very shoes she once despised
All too soon, she found herself standing
In the very shoes she once reviled

Looking into a mirror, she saw the very person
That she had once looked down upon
Looking into a mirror, she saw the very soul
That she had once counted as a candidate for hell
"Oh God, forgive me!" She felt shame, shame, shame

C. JoyBell C.

And remembered the first day of her birth
The way she once saw her destiny, her journey:
With untainted eyes, open and fixated!
With untainted eyes, transparent and free!
She remembered how it once was
How it should have always been
And saw how far away from that path she'd strayed
Her roots so far away

"I am nothing but a whore of holiness"
"Oh God, release me from my bonds!"
Step after painstaking step
Sojourning on the path of true light
The weight of the past years crumbled and fell
While she stepped closer and closer to the light
The veil over her eyes cracked like desert earth
It dissolved like useless dust
Each step taking her home, bringing her home
Until she finally stood back at her point of birth
Where all the memories returned
She saw through newborn eyes, once again
The rainbow in the horizon

The Chosen Ones

When the brightest light comes into your life and leaves
You will never again be able to see things clearly
Under the dim illuminations of the other ones

After the finest perfume of Ithaca
Has graced your neck and grazed your hair
How can you ever find the same fulfillment from less?

When a vibrant joy has flown into your life, like an entity
The scent and the taste of a higher dimension
How can you ever feel the same as before

After that joy has departed?

Some people are the brightest light
Some people are the finest perfume
Some people are the vibrant joy

Know how to see them
Know how to accept them
Know how to give and appreciate

Because when they leave

The whole world will be different

C. JoyBell C.

Everything Was Okay

I saw you
No, you don't understand

I really *did* see you
All on the inside like that

You held your chin high
So they would think you were proud

You swayed your hips just a little
So they'd think you were sophisticated

You tilted your head just the right way
So they could see your elegance

But you weren't proud– you were afraid
And that was okay

But you weren't sophisticated– not yet
You were still a child, and that was okay!

You were already elegant– yes
But you didn't need to be, not yet!

Thank you for looking into my eyes
Because I saw you, and you saw me

And everything was okay
And you've always had an honest laugh

We Are The Same

You saw me
No, You don't understand

You really *did* see me
All on the inside like that

I wanted them to think I was proud
So they couldn't hurt me

I wanted them to believe I was sophisticated
I didn't want to be just happy, anymore

I was elegant– yes
That was something they didn't have

I was afraid to be me
Behind the veil of what I thought they should see

But even beyond the veil–
That was still me!

Just not the honest me
Just not the one whom I love

Thank you for looking into my eyes
You saw me, and I saw you too

You gave me your eyes
And I've always had an honest laugh

C. JoyBell C.

Something Like The Humans

Why does the worn, torn look on your face
Tell me that everything in your life is going to be okay?
Isn't that contrary to what I should believe?

Why does the disarray of your disheveled hair
Call to my fingers
Like it's the most wondrous feeling in the world?

And how come your broken expectations
Make your soul shine more beautifully?
Shouldn't it be making you ugly?

The magnanimous weight of your future
Ravages your mind with fears and doubts
You didn't even shave this morning

How do I know that you're still beautiful?
Why is it that I think you're going to be okay?
Why do we love something like the humans?

I am never alone wherever I am. The air itself supplies me with a century of love. When I breathe in, I am breathing in the laughter, tears, victories, passions, thoughts, memories, existence, joys, moments, and the hues of the sunlight on many tones of skin; I am breathing in the same air that was exhaled by many before me. The air that bore them life. And so how can I ever say that I am alone?

The End

Closing Remarks

I feel grateful, and I thank all of you who read the things that I write and who take the time to let me know how you feel! When you're there, you are *really* there! And I feel as though I have been falling and getting up and falling and getting up again and learning and growing and flying right in front of your very eyes! I feel like all of you have nursed me in a way, and you don't even have any idea! In all my victories, and in my innumerous defeats, none of you knew what was going on; you were all just there, loving me! I am so thankful to God for your presence. *Thank you.*

My irreplaceable friend, Aileen Blanche, thank you for showing me that there is a goodness that still exists. You have shown me the face of God.

Benjie, you know I consider you my "fairy godmother," and I want to thank you truly, for being a rock for me and for showing me recently that there is a friendship that exists which is thicker than blood.

Last Christmas, I learned to appreciate the fact that I have a family, whom, even though we may have our great divides and huge differences, still forgive each other in the end! And I feel so thankful for that! For my family in the East Coast and in the South, I say thank you for reminding me of how beautiful Christmas can be!

God, you are my shield and my wine! Bless me, bless me, bless me!

A viaxe continúa!

May the sun forever snow upon your soul and her snowflakes melt into a crystal pool within your own heart that reflects the eagles flying above you, tall trees that dance in the winds, and your beautiful face when you kneel by the pool to stare in with eyes like glowing embers, full of the warmth of God and the angels. And as you kneel to look at your reflection, may you catch the glimpse of a star in the night Heavens from the corners of your eyes, to remind you that every night there is at least one candle that unendingly burns in the skies, for you! As you rise in the morning light, may the memories of your visions clothe you in both beauty and grace, enough to last a long lifetime!

Notes...
(Where you can draw your own dragonflies!)

I'm barely human. I'm more like a creature; to me, everything gives off a scent! Thoughts, moments, feelings, movements, words left unsaid, words barely spoken; they all have a distinct sense, distinct fragrances! Both a smell and a touch! To inhale is to capture, to experience! I can perceive and I can "touch" in so many odd ways! And so I am made up of all these scents, all these feelings! An illumination of nerve endings!

Notes...
(Where you can draw your own dragonflies!)

The one who is born of the earth, dreams of the sky.
The one who is born of the sky, dreams of the earth.

The main typeface in this book is set in 14 pt. *Perpetua*, by Eric Gill (1882- 1940) who was a British sculptor and stonecutter named *Royal Designer for Industry* by the *Royal Society of Arts* in London. The font itself was made to resemble hand-chiseled engravings, hence, who better to create such a feel for a font, than a sculptor and stonecutter?

"Perpetua may be judged in the small sizes to have achieved the object of providing a distinguished form for a distinguished text; and, in the large sizes, a noble, monumental appearance."

~ Stanley Morison

2034574R00081

Made in the USA
San Bernardino, CA
04 March 2013